Surfacing

Matthew Boyce

Presentation by *BookLeaf Publishing*

Web: www.bookleafpub.com

E-mail: info@bookleafpub.com

ISBN: 9789357745246

First edition 2023

This book is dedicated to my children. You are my life's greatest blessing and I love you more than words can express (and you know how long-winded your father is!). However, I will try anyway, with the help of someone who said it best...

Doubt thou the stars are fire; Doubt that the sun doth move; Doubt truth to be a liar; But never doubt I love. ~ William Shakespeare.

ACKNOWLEDGEMENT

There are many people I'd love to thank by name here that were a great encouragement throughout my journey, simply by being there for me. However, due to the nature of my writings, I won't name them here. Additionally, there are several in particular I'd like to extend a special thanks to. If it weren't for you, I can't imagine how I would have navigated this. You believed me when I felt no one else did. You know who you are and I will never forget.

PREFACE

This is not for everyone.

When I stumbled upon the opportunity to take this journey through poetry, I had no idea what I wanted it to look like. It didn't take long for me to realize that I wasn't at a place, mentally, where I could simply create as other poets often do. Instead, it dawned on me that I could use this to help my own healing process and, perhaps, even offer hope and understanding to others who have similar stories. I am recovering from what is called narcissistic abuse. I do not use that term lightly. As with many other conditions and terminology that become vogue, it has a tendency to be thrown around flippantly. However, the term is not as important as the behavior, which has existed for far longer and is most easily recognized by those who've lived it.

Over the course of several years, my children and I were on the receiving end of something I didn't understand at the time. It started so slowly and subtly, so much so that one would hardly recognize it. It began to steadily escalate once we were sufficiently attached. I would have never dreamed at the time that it could be intentional. I simply assumed that these were some sort of latent reactions to prior trauma that were surfacing in unhealthy ways. What else could it be? It would be crazy to think anyone would behave this way on purpose. I was made to feel like my perceptions and perspectives were not real. I knew I wasn't imagining things, and yet I found myself questioning what I could be missing. I became a shell of the man I was as they systematically disassembled me, piece by piece. I felt lost and confused as I desperately searched for an answer. One realization snapped everything into focus: this was intentional. Once I had awoken to this possibility, I tested it without ceasing. Behavior that had seemed so erratic to me suddenly became remarkably predictable.

Now, I need to make something clear, this is not a hit-piece. The intention is not to sling mud or to put anyone down. Admittedly, there are some truths from my life and personal experiences within that would seem harsh towards some. However, the purpose of sharing this is two-fold: first, writing has been a source of catharsis for me from a young age. It is uncommon, often even frowned upon, for men to emote in such ways. However, I think that writing can be a wonderful and even healthy way in which we can deal with negative emotions. When I read my poems, I am reminded of my days writing song lyrics as a teen. In my mind, the poems tend to reflect those dissonant rhythms and angst that characterized 90's hard rock.

Second, one of the most important parts of my healing has been coming to the realization that I am not alone. I have spent hundreds of hours to date studying narcissistic abuse. Connecting with others has helped me to process what occurred and given me the blessed reassurance that I was not crazy, that this is a pattern of behavior experienced by many others from various walks of life. This is no mere example of confirmation bias.

Now, as a Christian, I can imagine that some might misinterpret my intentions given such raw expressions of anger or bitterness in some of these poems and call me to forgiveness. Let me assure you that I have done just that. However, I feel it appropriate to also point out that the Bible does not shy away from difficult feelings and hurts. David provides many examples for us, one being found in Psalm 56:

5 All day long they twist my words;
all their schemes are for my ruin.

6 They conspire, they lurk,
 they watch my steps,
 hoping to take my life.

God doesn't like fake. Jesus consistently looked to the heart. We can be honest about our feelings, but it's what we do with them that matters. If we, as Christians, deny that these feelings exist, not only are we lying to ourselves but we create a stumbling block for believers who feel that they cannot live up to the "perfection" they see in others around them. Additionally, in situations where abuse is present, silence benefits the abuser and they count on the cover it provides. In the end, however, negative feelings should always point us back to our need for God.

Ultimately, I share these things so others might benefit. I experienced a myriad of emotions in response to something evil and I attempted to articulate those here. My hope is that through this expression, others might find comfort in knowing they are not alone and maybe find hope along the way. Jesus is that ultimate hope and if you don't know him, it is never too late.

This is my prayer for you.

Scattered Transmission
(Panic Attack)

Breathe in
I Help No You Have All
Breathe out
can me one are to rests
Breathe in
not I will so keep on
Breathe out
do can't believe very on my
Breathe in
this breathe you weak moving shoulders
Black out

Piece by Piece

Hello there, little fly.
How dare you disturb my peace?
You gracefully fluttered into MY web,
And now you plead for release?

Your wings, they are so pretty.
You should thank me for tying them down
Look friends, how beautiful!
What a gorgeous trespasser I've found!

Now, this will only hurt a little.
Ugh! Would you cease that crying?
I've only removed those gaudy wings,
And you act like you're dying!

You're welcome, by the way.
For all that I've sacrificed.
The goodies I planted to lure you here…
Trapping you in paradise!

Just look at all that I've given!
I have not emptied you, after all…
You still have enough left to suffer.
Question me?! What insolence! What gall!

Perhaps, I am just too merciful!
Perhaps, I have not taken enough!
Hold still while I tear off each one of your
legs…
Oh, why must you be so rough?

How could you call me cruel?
You mean you wish to stop me from feeling?
Somebody! Save me from this intruder!
Nevermind, that they're bleeding!

It's sad, you're so unforgiving!
I really do deserve better.
I've wasted far, far, too much time,
On just some worthless beggar.

You weren't so beautiful anyway.
It's really so easy to see.
By your dead cold eyes and broken wings…
That you always hated me.

Paroxysm

Dysfunction Junction
Anger meets fear, combustion
Wake of Destruction

Silent Night

The silent room speaks so loudly
No one can hear
The sound of breaking hearts
All around
The world sleeps so soundly
Blind to tears
Lives ripped apart

If tears grew hot with grief
They'd set fire to this place
Overcome this numbness
From one frozen heart's embrace
If you could hear a spirit weeping
The whole world would be awake

Lord, are you still listening?
Forgive me for my mistakes
I swear that I didn't know
This would take me further
Than I want to go
Drifting away
Paying so much more
Than I'd ever want to pay
Our love in vain
The silence always
Has so much to say

Beauty is the Beast

Fairytales forgot to mention
Myths and Legends failed to describe
Evil so subtle, Darkness so bright
Open up now, invite it inside
What luck! What Fortune!
May mercies never cease
Beware of its stare
Run, if you dare
Prey, pray
Beauty is the Beast

Sweet Poison

Hemlock and nightshade
One sweet sip
Easy going down
Always leads to
One bad trip
Never-ending
A spiral descending
The taste lingers on the lips
Reminding you
Every time you slip

Immovable

Oh! How presumptuous!
To assume I'd desire
The endorsement of snakes
The approval of liars
No, I won't admit
To crimes I did not commit
I've enough sins of my own
For those, I'll atone
If you will not believe me
Then just leave me alone

Muse

What once moved my heart to sing
Inspires it only to weep
Nothing fairer I could imagine
None more charming I could describe
Porcelain skin
Decaying within
Once, my muse
Whitewashed tomb

Serpentine

Liar, Liar
What's your desire?
All that they had was yours
Liar, Liar
Look what's transpired!
Lives set ablaze, but no more

An Honest Prayer

Dear Father,

There is so much I need to tell you.

The End.

Amen.

Minion

So many opinions
From one that doesn't know
Strength to weakness
Knowledge to hubris
Harm the innocent
Enable the malevolent
Content in ignorance
Oh, so arrogant!
Know not, the things you do
Know not, what you don't know
Unsuspecting minion

Take a Bow

The show is over
The curtains sway
The signal cuts and the
Whole world fades to gray
Kill the lights
Clear the stage
Pretend that everything will be the same
The crowd is gone now
Only ghosts drift in vain

No more sorrow
No more pain
You're forgiven
But the scars of your performance remain

Crestfallen

No more tears
Dry your eyes
Don't you know?
Boys don't cry
Broken toy
Grief-stricken
No remorse
Gift, ungiven

Façade

Once thought your heart a masterpiece
Painted by your pain
Hindsight reveals a grim disguise
A veil to hide your fangs
In solitude, I cannot help but miss
The façade that does not exist

03:00 AM

Silent city sleeping
Soles scraping on cement
Far-off engines
Only whispers hanging on a gentle wind
A breeze that dances
With night's sweet perfume
The lamppost's candlelight vigil
Beckons solemn souls
Down a neon path

An Honest Prayer pt. 2

Good morning, Lord
It's me
Never dreamed
That I'd be here again
Thought I was better
Thought I had learned
To that same old pile of vomit
I returned
Help me, Father
Take my hand
You are my strength
When I can barely stand

Remember Who You Are

The mirror cannot reconcile
The man I was
The man I am
The man I must become

Reflections reveal
Some stranger staring through the glass
But You break through the distortion
Reminding me where I stand
Strength made perfect in weakness
I am who You say I am

I can
I will
I MUST
I will not be defined
By the world
Or the deceptions of
A sinful mind
I will finish the race
Fall down seven
Get up eight

Arrows

Forgive me, Daughter
Forgive me, Sons
If there ever lived a fool
Then I've been one
How could I not notice?
How did I not see?
Only broken dreams and ill intentions
Seem to pursue me

I just want to say
In case I don't get the chance
Before God calls me away
That for you
There is no price too great
Nothing that I wouldn't trade
Re-live every hurt, even if I knew
You are proof
That God's promises are true
Every mess I made
Lead to you

Solace

What sweet respite found in darkness
What lachrymose beauty in pain
While waiting on the sun to rise
Take solace in the fireflies

Looking Forward

One day this all will end
One day I'll get it right
One day our hearts will mend
One day it won't be night
One day I will remember
One day I will forget
One day to be rendered
One day, but still, not yet

It Is Well

May the darkest of days
Lead me to hunger for your grace
For though today I may be broken
You remain unchanged
In your justice
In your mercy
In your love
If I draw another breath
I'll use it to praise you
If I die before I wake
Use my story for your glory
Whatever shattered parts remain
They are yours
Scars and all